LEADING WITH CONFIDENCE

HOW TO LEAD AND DEVELOP OTHERS WITH CONFIDENCE

Leading With Confidence

How To Lead and Develop Others With Confidence

By
Miranda Burnette

Keys to Success Publishing
Atlanta, GA

Leading With Confidence: How To Lead and Develop Others With Confidence

ISBN: 978-0999893821

P. O. Box 314

Clarkdale, GA 30111

www.mirandaburnetteministries.org

Keys to Success Publishing

Atlanta, GA 30127

Cover Design by Jackie Moore

DEDICATION

I dedicate this book, *Leading With Confidence,* to Tiffany Carter. Tiffany, you are truly a powerful, strong leader with great confidence. Keep on allowing God to use you to touch and make an impact on the lives of many. Continue to inspire, encourage, and be the dynamic motivator that you are. May God bless you, CONFIDENT LEADER, to reach your goals and to make all of your dreams a reality. THE SKY IS THE LIMIT!

TABLE OF CONTENTS

INTRODUCTION

Confidence is about believing in yourself, feeling good about yourself, and feeling confident about your abilities. Being a confident leader is about having a "Can-Do" attitude and believing that you can reach your goals and achieve great things.

This book is about being yourself, having confidence to be who you are, and leading others confidently. It is about being the unique individual God created you to be. If you are a leader, never try to hide your uniqueness. Instead, be thankful for it. Don't be afraid to be you. Be yourself. Who else is better qualified?

Always be a first-rate version of yourself, instead of a second-rate version of somebody else.

A leader with confidence will accomplish more than a leader without confidence. When we find out who we are in the Lord and become secure in that knowledge, we don't have to try to be somebody we are not, and we don't have to go around comparing ourselves to others.

Instead of focusing on what others have, focus on what makes you who you are. We don't have to put others down to make ourselves look good. Until you learn to accept who you are and work to address your flaws, you will never grow as a leader.

Ralph Waldo Emerson said, "The creation of a thousand forests is in one acorn."

It doesn't matter where you are right now in life, you can grow to be someone great. In addition, you can also help many other people grow to reach their full potential.

Galatians 5:1 (KJV) says, "Stand fast therefore in the liberty wherewith Christ hath made us free, and be not entangled again with the yoke of bondage.

Walk in your freedom in Christ. We are free to be ourselves in Christ. Relax and be yourself. Be happy with who you are. God made you an original, not a copy.

Ethel Waters said, "I know I'm somebody, 'cause God don't make no junk."

Don't try to be like someone else. Each individual has different strengths and weaknesses. The word individual means separate, distinguished by specific attributes or identifying traits, distinct or unique. Don't try to be someone you are not. If you be yourself, in spite of your flaws, we all have them, people will respect you more. It takes courage to be yourself. Be a courageous leader.

Be the best you, you can be. You are one of a kind. You are valuable to God.

Luke 12:7 (ESV) says, "Why, even the hairs of your head are all numbered. Fear not; you are of more value than many sparrows.

God is for you, and he wants you to be for you too. A quote by an unknown author says this:

If you really put a small value upon yourself, rest assured that the world will not raise your price.

__Author Unknown

Are you for yourself or against yourself? Zig Ziglar said this:

"You can't consistently perform in a manner inconsistent with the way you see yourself."

__Zig Ziglar

Know who you are in Christ. True leadership involves who you are or who you are becoming, as opposed to what you do. Who you are consists of how you think and what you value.

Proverbs 23:7 (NKJV) says, "For as he thinks in his heart, so is he..."

To be a great leader, you have to believe you are a great leader. God always focuses on our inward qualities or our heart. God is concerned about our character, which is who we are. Our character has more to do with who we are on the inside rather than who we present ourselves to be on the outside. Our character is who we are when no one is looking.

Our character and inward qualities take time to develop in our lives. However, as they develop, our confidence as a leader increases and our attitude becomes more positive because our attitude and confidence as a leader are related.

To be an effective leader, it starts with integrity of the heart. Integrity is more important than ability. You can train a person to do the job, but if the person doesn't have integrity, you have a problem on your hands.

Integrity means firm adherence to a code of especially moral or artistic values, an unimpaired condition, the quality or state of being complete or undivided *(Merriam Webster).* Integrity also means being the same inside and outside. It means your actions match your words, and you will do what you said you would do.

Philippians 4:13 (AMPC) says, "I have strength for all things in Christ Who empowers me [I am ready for anything and equal to anything through Him Who infuses inner strength into me; I am self-sufficient in Christ's sufficiency].

We are self -sufficient in Christ's sufficiency. Whatever we do, we do it through Christ.

Philippians 4:13 (NKJV) says, "I can do all things through Christ who strengthens me."

Your confidence must come from God. You are not sufficient by yourself. Remember; don't try to be like someone else. Be the leader God has called you to be. Lead the way God wants you to lead. Put your trust in God, and lean and depend on Him. Don't try to do it in your own ability, but in God's ability and strength.

You CAN do all things; even lead with confidence,

through Christ. Therefore, in order to be that dynamic leader you would like to be, start LEADING WITH CONFIDENCE today!

CHAPTER 1

CHARACTERISTICS OF A CONFIDENT LEADER

"A true leader has the confidence to stand alone, the courage to make tough decisions, and the compassion to listen to the needs of others. He does not set out to be a leader, but becomes one by the quality of his actions and the integrity of his intent."

__General Douglas Macarthur

What is your idea of a confident and effective leader? Is it someone who has the ability to remain calm under pressure, give people clear directives, and inspire others? Does leadership involve being forceful and direct, or one or the other? Being a leader involves more than the things I've just mentioned. Everyone comes to the table with their own idea of what a leader is, and often, that perception is shaped by past experiences, beliefs, and the influence of someone who was once in a position of leadership over them.

WHAT IS CONFIDENCE?

Confidence is an essential characteristic for leaders. The word confidence, according to *Webster* means trust or faith, a feeling of assurance, especially self-assurance or security. Confidence in the *Greek* means a quality of assurance that leads one to under-take a thing. It means a belief that you are able and acceptable. Confidence causes one to be bold, open, or plain.

Confidence is having faith in yourself, and belief in your abilities without any arrogance or conceit. Someone with confidence doesn't put others down in order to lift him or herself up. A confident person is secure enough to give credit where credit is due without being intimidated. Confidence is vital to our leadership success. It is crucial if you are going to accomplish anything in life. It is an important part of our being. That is why the writer of Hebrews urges us in the following verse not to throw away our confidence. Don't throw your confidence away!

Hebrews 10:35 (NIV) says, "So do not throw away your confidence; it will be richly rewarded.

Leadership is more than a title or position. Many people hold high positions in an organization, but are not effective or confident leaders. Confidence is a key to creating a positive working environment.

True leadership is marked by influence, faithfulness, and ability. Leaders must walk in love, have a servant's heart, take the initiative, and judge themselves honestly. Once these characteristics are cultivated in your life, you are on your way to becoming a leader who is fit for the Master's use.

Influence is probably one of the most important characteristics of a true leader. Influence is having the ability to motivate others to follow you. Most natural-born leaders possess the innate ability to persuade people to follow them. Something about them gets people's attention and makes them want to go in the same direction. If you are looking for potential leaders to serve in an organization, look for the individuals' potential to influence and motivate others.

As a confident leader, your faithfulness will be tested regularly. *Webster's* definition of faithfulness is supportive, loyal, worthy of trust or belief, consistent, constant, firm, resolute, steadfast, and true. Take a look at your own life and your commitment to a particular thing. Are you loyal, trustworthy, and steadfast in the things of God, as well as the other responsibilities God has placed in your charge? Are you willing to consistently carry out your tasks and responsibilities over a long period of time, even when the going gets tough? Have you stuck it out when you felt like quitting? If your answer to these questions is yes, and you are actively demonstrating faithfulness, you are preparing yourself to be an effective confident leader. God is looking for men and women who will be faithful, confident leaders and do what they have been called to do. He needs leaders He can count on to carry out His plans, and influence others to do the same.

Another quality of a confident leader is ability. Faithfulness is critical, yet there must also be demonstrated ability in the life of a leader. You can be faithful, but if you don't possess the ability to carry out specific tasks, you won't be effective and your confidence will be tested.

Some people have natural, effortless abilities, while others do not. For example, you may be naturally good with administrative tasks, or you may be a quick thinker who has the ability to solve problems easily, more so than someone else. Maybe you can give directions clearly, or have another skill that serves you well as a leader, and is easy for you to perform.

 Certain abilities can be developed with the proper training, if they don't come naturally, to help you become a more confident leader. Public speaking, for example, can be developed through practice. If you have identified that foundational area of being able to influence others, and know that you have leadership qualities, but need to develop in a particular area; seek out the necessary training; ask questions and seek information and people who can mentor you and help sharpen your skills.

As you practice each of these characteristics in your life, you will gain great confidence in your leadership and be well on your way to being the effective, confident leader you desire to be. Confidence is contagious. If you are a strong, confident leader, you will not only possess the power you need, but you will influence your followers and empower them to be confident leaders, as well. Therefore, you will be equipping them to accomplish great things in their lives, and you will be equipping them to be all they can be.

CHAPTER 2

A CONFIDENT LEADER GETS RESULTS

"A good leader inspires people to have confidence in the leader. A great leader inspires people to have confidence in themselves."

__Eleanor Roosevelt

Effective leaders produce results. It is the leader's responsibility to make things happen because others are depending on him. The measure of success is demonstrated when you, the leader, is not present. How smoothly your organization runs when you are not around is a reflection of your true leadership ability. It shows how well you have trained and imparted your vision and objectives into the hearts of your staff.

One major hindrance to having a successful organization is being a leader who has what my pastor calls *The Octopus Mentality*. This is when you feel you must have your hands in everything. Because of the personal pride you take in believing nothing can successfully happen without your direction, you hinder the growth and leadership potential of others who could do the job, and make things easier for you.

Whenever you feel you *must* be involved or things won't work without you, you actually block your own promotion. But when you train others to do their jobs in excellence, and give them the liberty to make mistakes, you demonstrate your own leadership skills. Recognize that you cannot do everything by yourself, and you do not have to be involved in every detail of every department for it to be successful.

ORIENTATION AND TRAINING

One of the main reasons failure occurs in

leadership is lack of proper orientation and training. It is not enough to assume people will absorb the full scope of knowledge for their jobs. When they are not successful in their positions, they are labeled the wrong person for the job. That is not fair. The problem is they were not effectively trained and equipped to do their job.

Orientation and training go together. To *orient* means to make them familiar with something. This part of the process involves getting the person accustomed to their new environment, their position, and walking them through the process as they are growing into a confident leader. However, it doesn't stop there.

Once you initially orient someone with the basics; then and only then does the training begin. Ninety days is a standard time period to train and evaluate your trainee's progress. It is also enough time for strengthening their confidence. However, do not be discouraged if it takes longer. Make sure whatever period you allocate for training is full of valuable time spent informing your trainee about every aspect and responsibility of leadership. Prepare them for all the possible scenarios that could take place, and make sure they know how to handle pressure situations with confidence.

A confident leader recognizes what he or she needs, and then hires based on those needs. In some ways as a leader, you must take a hands-off approach; while it may not be as comfortable having total trust in another's ability early on, you must make the decision not to micromanage every aspect of their progress; or the progress of those under them. Remember, part of operating as a confident leader is also having the confidence in yourself and your selective decisions.

Do you have an effective way of properly training the people who become a part of your organization? Are you equipping them for future success and responsibility in your absence, or by not having the proper confidence-builders in place, equipping them for failure? When a person is capable of performing their job, they will be successful. It is up to you, the leader, to make sure that knowledge is effectively imparted and executed to boost their confidence.

Results are seen when your objectives are met, and your vision is fulfilled. You don't have to have the *Octopus Mentality* to get things done. God will send skilled people to you, but you must pull their potential out of them through sound training and orientation, while simultaneously creating a safety net to catch them when they make mistakes.

Remember the power of influence; it is your responsibility to use influence to propel those under your direction to higher standards of excellence. Constantly consider different and better ways of doing things; get people on your team who can contribute to ideas, and begin to think the same way. You have the power to mold leaders, which can take your organization to the next level. Utilize that ability to be a leader who gets God-given results!

CAN YOU RELATE?

Are you a confident leader who gives directives and make things happen but lack relational skills? It is not enough to be a mover and a shaker from a professional standpoint, if you fail to master the art of dealing with others in a way that gets results and secures their loyalty, you may compromise your own confidence. The question is, *can you relate*?

There are simple ways to build strong connections with your staff. Sometimes the little things make the biggest difference. For example, call each person into your office at some point, and speak to him or her one-on-one about non work-related issues. Ask them about themselves and their personal goals. Learn something unique about each staff member and keep the lines of communication open. Your genuine interest communicates more confidence to them and their abilities.

The more you present yourself as an approachable leader; it will instill a greater level of confidence in you. In other words, be approachable and have an open door policy. People will feel more comfortable opening up to you on a more personal level. Maintaining this type of interaction eliminates the fear that if they make a mistake, you will be inflexible and harsh.

Create an atmosphere of care in your company, and that atmosphere should be extended toward every staff member, on every team, in every department. You will get better results from those who work for you when they feel you are genuinely in their corner and care about them.

"Nobody cares how much you know, until they know how much you care,"

__Theodore Roosevelt

THE BIG THREE

Being knowledgeable, consistent, and responsible are three areas that will set you on the course to successful, confident leadership, and garner the respect of the people who serve you. Know the areas you oversee, know your staff, and know how those staff members will respond in certain situations that arise.

Have a full working knowledge of the different positions you oversee. It is your responsibility to educate yourself about processes and procedures, in case questions or concerns arise. You are held accountable for what goes on in your department or company. The more you remain aware, the more confident you are when having to respond to those in authority over you.

Being knowledgeable also means you are keenly aware of your staff's strengths and weaknesses. Over time, you will begin to see where they excel, and where they fall short; you can make adjustments to help them improve, grow, and develop.

Consistency is another "big three." How consistent are you in your own life? Are you disciplined in prayer and the study of God's Word?

13

What about your diet, exercising, managing your finances, and sowing into the Kingdom of God? Being disciplined and consistent in the little things positions you for the bigger things. When you are strongly discerning in God's Word and His voice, you can manage daily business with surety and confidence.

There is the area of responsibility; first to God, and then to those we oversee as leaders. You must be responsible for what you start, what you say, what you demonstrate, and what you put out. Will you accept responsibility when things go wrong, even accepting the blame if necessary?

Responsibility with the words you speak is especially important. Be mindful of what and how you say things, and strive to always speak in line with God's Word. Use wisdom in your speech, and be an example of God's character in everything you do and say.

CHAPTER 3

CONFIDENT LEADERS REPRODUCE CONFIDENT LEADERS

"At its core, I believe leadership is about instilling confidence in others."

__Howard Schultz

Are you confident enough to thoroughly practice what you preach? Do you walk the talk, or are you just a big talker? Confident leaders must model the desired behavior to those who follow them. As the confident leader, you must demonstrate the qualities you want to see in others.

The way you dress either enhances or hinders your confidence. It also sends a message of professionalism to those you encounter and arouses a sense of respect. Not everyone feels strongly about adhering to certain dress codes, but it is a wonderful standard to set for those who work and serve at your company in a professional capacity.

I strive to demonstrate to others what I want to see in them. I learned this from my pastor who most times is in a suit and tie when he preaches or ministers. Confident leaders carry themselves a certain way; therefore, they are effective in leading by example.

Leading by example is not just done where exterior appearances are concerned, but more importantly, with character and integrity. If you want to lead people who walk in the love of God, have high moral standards, and demonstrate God's character in what they do, it must start with you. Granted, every person has a free will to make their own decisions, but your decision to live the principles of God's Word creates a standard others will want to follow.

How do you act when you are leading others? Do you engage in backbiting, gossip and other negative behaviors? These negative behaviors can greatly impact your confidence and ability to be effective. But why would such actions be a part of any leader's conduct? These are questions you must explore in order to resolve them to begin to operate effectively and with confidence. Ask yourself; why would anyone want to follow a leader who is defeated in their own personal life, or act in a way that doesn't reflect God's true character?

The Bible gives clear guidelines, which dictate how confident leaders should conduct themselves. By aligning your life with these standards, you position yourself to have people follow you who operate the same way.

2 Timothy 2:24 (AMP) says, "The servant of the Lord must not participate in quarrels, but must be kind to everyone [even-tempered, preserving peace, and he must be], skilled in teaching, patient and tolerant when wronged."

Proverbs 16:12 (MSG) says, "Good leaders abhor wrongdoing of all kinds; sound leadership has a moral foundation."

Proverbs 29:12 (MSG) says, "When a leader listens to malicious gossip, all the workers get infected with evil."

17

Proverbs 16:15 (MSG) says, "Good-tempered leaders invigorate lives; they're like spring rain and sunshine."

Anyone can follow these guidelines, and be successful as a confident leader in their particular area. Most importantly, these behaviors please God. If you want others to follow you, you must strive to be a good example! One who is confident, grounded, and effective in allowing others to follow. This requires walking in the love of God and according to His Word. Your followers will pattern their lives after what they see you do. And when they see you giving glory to God through your lifestyle, radiating confidence, and reaping the rewards that come with it, they will want to experience the same results. It is simply not enough to be a big talker; you must walk your talk. Live a life worthy of having, while operating in confidence; you too will see that others will follow you.

If you were to go several days without eating food, you would feel the effects in your body. You may become weak, and your mind may not be able to think clearly. The same thing happens spiritually, when you neglect time spent with God in prayer and in the Word of God. As a confident leader, one of the keys to your success is maintaining contact with your Heavenly Father daily.

How else will you be able to make wise decisions that contribute to the success of your organization? Without the guidance of the Holy Spirit, everything you do will ultimately fail, and cost you time, money, and energy.

Surprisingly, many may wonder how to maintain daily contact with God. The answer is simple; through Bible study, regular prayer, and praising God. These are vital components to keeping your relationship with the Father fresh and flourishing and will help you, as a leader, know God's will and to fulfill it. These components position you to receive the insight you need as an effective and confident leader.

CHAPTER 4

GOD'S WORD + PRAYER = CONFIDENCE

"When the leader lacks confidence, the followers lack commitment."

__John Maxwell

It is essential in operating as a confident leader to spend time daily with God by reading His Word. The Word is the spiritual food you need to keep you operating in *confidence overflow.* Remain full of the Word at all times, so you will have the spiritual strength, wisdom, and discernment to hear and follow the voice of the Lord. Doing this will also counter the enemy's attacks against you.

When you neglect personal time spent in God's Word, you actually starve your spirit and lower your defenses against negative things that may try to sidetrack you, like depression, negative emotional reactions, offense, and frustration. These things greatly affect your ability to remain confident in leadership.

The Bible says the joy of the Lord is your strength (Nehemiah 8:10). It is the joy that comes from what you know from God's Word that will allow you to maintain peace in the midst of turmoil and remain confident in the midst of trials and tribulation. However, for your *joy tank* to be full, as a confident leader, be sure to spend a significant amount of time in God's Word. It is your spiritual substance and should not be neglected.

Meditate on the Word of God to maintain your confidence-connection with the Father. Reading the Bible is one thing, but when you take time to ponder and intensely think about each Scripture, and how it applies to your life, that you get even more spiritual strength, understanding, and confidence from it.

Have you ever noticed that the more time you spend meditating on a thing you begin to envision it? It seems to become more real, more reachable, and more tangible. The same thing holds true when it comes to meditating on God's Word. This is because spending time in meditation and confessing the Word out loud boosts your confidence in every area of your life. Turning Scriptures over in your mind will help you receive the spiritual nourishment from them. God will begin to speak to you through His Word, when it becomes infused in your spirit through regular meditation.

Through this, you become confident that He guides and directs you to do according to His will. When you are sure that God has ordained you to start a ministry, open a business, or to make some type of big investment, there is a peace and a keen level of confidence that accompanies you on your journey.

Additionally, prayer is communication with God, which also feeds and strengthens your confidence. The more you know about God, the more you are aware of His abilities and the more you trust Him. When you engage in dialogue between you and the Father in which you both speak and listen to one another, it only boosts your trust and confidence in what He has called you to do.

Effective prayer is a combination of listening to God, praising God, and praying the Word of God by speaking it aloud, echoing to God what He has already declared. As a leader, you should have the confidence in knowing that when you take an issue to God in prayer, that He hears you.

Praying the Word of God is also effective because of the power contained in the Scriptures. When you declare what God has already said in His written Word, you are absolutely certain to get results because His Word does not return to Him void (Isaiah 55:11); He will *always* bring to pass what He has said.

If your prayer and Word time has fallen short, it is time to get back on track. The number of people who follows you as a leader is connected to the anointing you possess. God has equipped you to carry out His vision, yet you must maintain daily contact, which strengthens your spirit and positions you to receive His power, wisdom, guidance and direction; therefore, setting you up to be a confident leader.

BEING A SUPPORTIVE CONFIDENT LEADER

No matter what position of leadership you hold,

your success is largely based on your faithfulness to another person's vision. Who you are connected to, and who you sow into as a leader determines how high you will go in your own ministry, business, or career.

You must develop a sense of loyalty to another leader who has imparted into your life, and who has a vision from God. When you are faithful with helping support the increase of another person's ministry, business, or vision, God will set you up to have the same success.

The spiritual principle of seedtime and harvest is the foundation for this. *Genesis 8:22 (NKJV) says,*

"While the earth remains, Seedtime and harvest, Cold and heat, Winter and summer, And day and night Shall not cease."

Galatians 6:7 (ESV) says, "Do not be deceived: God is not mocked, for whatever one sows, that will he also reap."

Whatever seeds you sow toward the success of someone else will eventually come back to you. In addition, confident leaders are mindful of their words, and avoid speaking against those in authority over them. When you are confident, you have no need to operate in such a manner.

Divine order is the prerequisite for miracles, and when you operate according to God's order, and respect the spiritual principles of seedtime and harvest as it pertains to building confidence in those you lead, your increase is assured. Support those who are successful at what you want to accomplish, and God will allow the same blessings to flow through to you from your leadership.

CHAPTER 5

DEVELOPING YOUR LEADERSHIP CONFIDENCE

"The trust of the people in the leaders reflects the confidence of the leaders in the people."

__Paulo Freire

God wants Christians who are willing to be used as leaders. Those who God uses are not always the most talented, but those who have the best attitude and allow God to prepare them. Sometimes the things that God tells us to do in order to prepare and promote us, we may not like or want to do. But if we want God to use us, it will require obedience. We may think we are doing great in a particular area, but God may want to develop us more in that area.

Whether we like it or not, if we want God to use us we must work with Him to develop our leadership skills. God might tell you to go to school for four years or attend a weekly speech class. Are you willing to develop and maximize your potential in this area to be used by God?

You may feel that you don't need to go to school, take a speech class, or spend hours studying in a particular area to be used by God. However, before God uses anyone He prepares and equips them. Leading you to go to school or to take speech classes, may be the way God desires to equip you. To be used as a confident leader, we eventually will have to yield to God's will.

As a leader, right now you may not be where you would like to be in your level of confidence and overall effectiveness. You may want to reach your full leadership potential *now*. And you can! You can learn to reach your goals and fulfill God's plan for your life just by your willingness to be used by God.

A confident leader is not necessarily someone who has a large organization or is in a position that influences thousands of people. A confident leader is someone who is on top of things in his or her realm of influence. If you want to operate in your full leadership potential, start where you are, regardless if you feel everything is perfect or not. Do something now. Nobody starts at the finish line. Don't despise the day of small beginnings *(Zechariah 4:10).*

Allow God to develop you into the dynamic confident leader He has chosen you to be, and accomplish great things for His glory.

CHAPTER 6

FOLLOW THE LEADER

"Leadership is the capacity and will to rally men and women to a common purpose and the character which inspires confidence."

_Bernard Montgomery

Many of us make our own plans and ask God to bless them, but we should ask God to give us a plan and direct us on how to carry out His plan, His way, and in His timing.

A man's heart plans his way, But the Lord directs his steps.

_ *Proverbs 16:9 (NKJV)*

We should make plans --counting on God to direct us.
_ *Proverbs 16:9 (TLB)*

Have you ever played the game, *Follow the Leader? Follow the Leader* is a familiar game that is played and enjoyed by children all over the world. The rules for this game are, you choose a leader, and you follow him wherever he goes and does whatever he does. You want to make sure you follow the leader exactly and that you are not a quitter.

In our own lives as adults, we also play *Follow the Leader.* We follow leaders at church, at school, in sports, in our government, and in other areas of our lives. We have to make sure we choose a leader who will lead us in the right direction. We have a Leader who we can depend on to always lead us in the right direction. The Leader that is guaranteed to lead us right without fail is the Holy Spirit.

Many times in our lives, we believe that we know the solution to a problem without a doubt, but if we will just seek God about it and listen to the Holy Spirit, it will most likely turn out to be the opposite of what we thought it would be. God knows what is best. God is God and He sees the big picture. We think we know! That is why we need to be led by the

Holy Spirit, especially if we are leaders.

Proverbs 21:2 says, "Every way of a man is right in his own eyes, but the Lord weighs the hearts.

The Holy Spirit is our Teacher, and the Word of God says that He will lead and guide us into all truth.

But when the Spirit of truth comes, He will guide you into all truth. For He will not speak on His own authority. But He will speak whatever He hears, and He will tell you things that are to come.

__John 16:13 (MEV)

The Holy Spirit only speaks what He hears the Father says. Whatever the Holy Spirit leads you to do always lines up with the written Word of God. Being led by the Holy Spirit is an assured way to achieve victory and success in your everyday life. Being led by the Holy Spirit will keep you out of a lot of trouble and from making numerous of mistakes that you will regret later. When you listen to the Holy Spirit and obey His voice, it will save you time, money, and wasted energy doing things that are not God's will for your life.

If you are a Christian, the Holy Spirit resides in your born-again spirit. As you renew your mind with the Word of God and recognize the voice of the Holy

Spirit in your life, the Holy Spirit will lead you into a life of abundance, peace, joy, protection, and success. In order to recognize the voice of the Holy Spirit, we must spend time in the Word of God and in prayer.

There are many decisions we have to make in life that will lead us to success or failure. There are so many choices to make and so many paths in life we could choose such as what job to take, what schools to attend, where to attend church, who to marry, choosing the right friendships, or even how to deal with everyday situations in our lives. So it is vitally important that we are able to hear God's voice and follow the leading of the Holy Spirit along the way. We need to stop and acknowledge God in all things.

Proverbs 3:5-6 (AMPC) says, "Lean on, trust in, and be confident in the Lord with all your heart and mind and do not rely on your own insight or understanding. In all your ways know, recognize, and acknowledge Him, and He will direct and make straight and plain your paths."

The Bible tells us in *John 14:16 (AMPC)* that the Holy Spirit is our Comforter.

And I will ask the Father, and He will give you another Comforter (Counselor, Helper, Intercessor, Advocate, Strengthener, and Standby), that He may remain with

32

you forever—

From studying the Word of God, I have come to understand that the Holy Spirit is our Teacher, Guide, Comforter, Counselor, Helper, Intercessor, Advocate, Strengthener, and Standby. How do we follow the Leader, the Holy Spirit? First, we must yield and submit to His leadership. We must be willing and obedient, even when we don't always know where He is leading us. We must trust Him completely. We cannot allow circumstances or other people to change our course. We must continue to follow the Leader.

Second, we need to understand that the Holy Spirit speaks to the spirit part of us. Man is a tri-part being—spirit, soul, and body. *(1 Thessalonians 5:23).* You are a spirit being who has a soul and lives in a body.

Third, we must renew our minds with the Word of God so that we will recognize His voice. How does the Holy Spirit lead us? There are different ways God can speak to us. He leads us by an inward witness or a still-small voice, through peace, other people, circumstances, wisdom, prophecy, dreams, visions, His Word, or an audible voice *(It's not often that an audible voice happens, but it does happen today).* The

Holy Spirit can impact our lives in a dynamic way when we choose to follow Him. The Holy Spirit can lead and guide us into God's perfect plan and will for our lives.

As leaders, in order to be a great leader, we have to follow the Leader of Leaders, God. God is our Role Model. The Leader of all leaders is God: The Ultimate Leader. God gives us power to lead, that power is the power of the Holy Spirit. Start following the Leader, the Holy Spirit today, and watch your confidence to leader others soar!

CHAPTER 7

GROWING AS A CONFIDENT LEADER

"The leader demonstrates confidence that the challenge can be met, the need resolved, the crisis overcome."

__John Haggai

An organization can only go as far as the leadership. If you are not growing or making progress, your organization will become stagnant. Leaders who aren't maturing will oversee others who aren't moving to the next level.

Growth and maturity are essential. Other people

suffer when you have not dealt with emotional problems, or if your spiritual life is not on point. When you lack in confidence or feel out of control in your own life, most likely you will attempt to control other people with the absence of these essentials. This leads to stressful relationships with others. It then becomes vital that you deal with these issues through God's Word so you can move to your next level.

Effective leadership involves relational skills. How you present information to others makes the difference in how it is received. You can be firm, at the same time, deal with issues without being mean and harsh. The key is in your level of confidence and delivery.

Be direct and honest, but make sure your heart is in the right place. You should never be afraid to confront the things that concern you. Remember, your objective is to help others understand your expectations and clearly communicate what they need to do to meet those objectives.

You can be the confident leader God has called you to be by developing in the area of relational skills. By using God's Word as your guide and allowing the Holy Spirit to teach you how to interact with others, you will develop loyal followers who can carry out your vision in excellence.

CHARACTER, SERVANTHOOD, AND LOVE

God created you with character to lead others with a servant's heart. Without these two things, it is difficult to be the type of leader who pleases God and has enduring success. A confident leader *must* first, and foremost, be a servant.

Sometimes people think of servanthood as the last thing to consider when they are in a leadership position. However, Jesus says that servanthood is actually the distinguishing mark of a person who wants to lead. In Matthew 23:11 (KJV) He also says,

"But he that is greatest among you shall be your servant."

Clearly, Jesus put a high priority on leaders being servants. In *Mark 9:35 (KJV)* He says,

"... If any man desires to be first, the same shall be last of all, and servant of all."

A servant is willing to do whatever is necessary to be a blessing to others. It is the leader who goes above and beyond what is asked of him, not because he or she *has* to, but because they *want* to. This leader is not concerned with being recognized; instead, it is simply to please God. The leader who has a servant's heart has released selfishness, and is consumed with meeting the needs of people; even if he or she has to be inconvenienced.

What makes a leader want to serve others? The love of God! Walking in love enables a leader to serve others even when they do not feel like it.

As an evangelist with a teaching ministry, and the founder of *Miranda Burnette Ministries*, I consider myself a servant; I have the same expectation of servanthood from every leader that may come under my charge. No one is above the call to serve others, regardless of their title.

Every time I speak, teach, or write books, I have a message to deliver to God's people. I am not just carrying a title; I am *serving* every person present or listening by seeking God on how to be an effective and confident leader.

A true servant serves where there is a need. The servant takes ownership of *any* area that has a need to be filled. Instead of waiting to be told what to do, a servant acts with purpose and confidence.

To have a servant's heart, means to embrace the character of God, and begin to think as He does.

38

God's primary concern is for people. As a confident leader, you must adopt the same passion for people.

You cannot be an effective and confident leader without the fruit of the Spirit operating in your life. For instance, there is no excuse for meanness or acting in an ungodly way. As confident leaders, we must be sure we are operating with the right spirit, and reflecting the love of Jesus Christ at all times. Nothing says confidence like the love of God flowing in and through our lives. The impression you leave people with will stand out in their minds. Strive to leave an impression of confidence, love, and concern for them.

Be willing to examine yourself in these areas. Evaluate your confidence level: and whether you are loving, kind, gentle and patient with others. Are you faithful; demonstrating self-control? Remember, the Holy Spirit is willing to help you develop in the love of God, when you are obedient to God's Word.

The ingredients of true leadership are character, love, influence, attitude, faithfulness, and servanthood. If you make a quality decision to locate and cultivate these qualities in your life, you develop in confidence and become a leader who fulfills the call in excellence and impact people in a powerful way!

CHAPTER 8

LEADING WITH CONFIDENCE

"The history of the world is full of men who rose to leadership, by sheer force of self-confidence, bravery and tenacity."

__Mahatma Gandhi

Confidence plays a significant role in leadership. Confidence is a key to success in leadership. Confidence is the foundation of leadership. The leader must have this strong foundation to be able to transfer it to his or her followers. It is only with confidence that you, as a leader, will be able to provide a foundation for your followers.

You are that solid rock upon which your followers are depending on to be the example they need to grow and develop as leaders. Followers need to see the stability in their leader and they are looking for you to produce the stability that they might not have themselves. Confidence is an essential quality of leadership on which all the other qualities of leadership depends or is based.

A leader can be taught many of the characteristics we have discuss in this book and many other fundamentals of leadership. However, if the leader does not have confidence in him or herself, effective leadership will not exist. A leader who is highly qualified and have many skills, but lacks confidence, will have a difficult time leading others.

Francisco Dao says, "Self-confidence is the fundamental basis from which leadership grows. Trying to teach leadership without first building confidence is like building a house on a foundation of sand. It may have a nice coat of paint, but it is ultimately shaky at best."

Leadership confidence is a more crucial asset than knowledge, skill, or experience. Without confidence, a leader will find it hard to make difficult decisions, lead with authority, communicate

41

effectively with others, or to take smart risks. Confidence is what separates average leaders from great leaders. Don't allow a lack of confidence to hold you back!

To become the leader you've always wanted to be, lead with confidence. If there were one quality that would make you successful in motivating people to follow you, it would be confidence. Confidence makes others believe in us. People can sense confidence. They can also recognize a lack of confidence.

When others can see that you lack conviction, they will be far less likely to trust in your leadership. As you learned in the previous chapters in this book, confidence plays a vital role in your ability to lead others. Confidence is a key to effective leadership. Your ability to exhibit confidence will have a noticeable impact on your ability to lead effectively. If you want to lead others effectively, you must believe in your abilities to lead and succeed. You must display confidence in everything that you do. Effective leaders utilize the trait of confidence.

You can improve your confidence as a leader by knowing your job as well as possible. To do this, familiarize yourself with the skills that lead to effective leadership and your confidence will improve dramatically. As a leader, you can build confidence in others by recognizing their accomplishments. You can focus more on their strengths than on their weaknesses.

Becoming an excellent leader is a process. Leadership takes time, effort, and information. Developing into an exceptional, confident leader depends on skills that can't be developed over night, but for those who put in the time and effort that is required, they can be developed overtime. Good leaders are good because they want to be and they work on what it takes to be great every day. If you continue to invest in your leadership development, you will overtime eventually grow into the outstanding, confident leader you desire to be!

ABOUT THE AUTHOR

MIRANDA BURNETTE is the president and founder of Miranda Burnette Ministries, Inc. She is a licensed evangelist. She is also the founder of Keys to Success Academy, Inc., a Conference Line Leadership Bible School where she teaches people how to discover and fulfill their calling, to make their dreams a reality, to be successful in every area of their lives, and to be all God created them to be. The vision of Miranda Burnette Ministries is to educate, equip, and empower others to be successful leaders and reach their full God-given potential.

Miranda is the author of *Success Starts in Your Mind, Dare to Dream and Soar like an Eagle, Leader to Leader, Keys to Living a Fruit-Filled Life, Dare to Dream Again—Book and Study Guide, and Winning With the Power of Love— Book and Study Guide.* She also makes an impact on the lives of others with her teachings on CD.

She is the founder and president of I Can Christian Academy, Inc. Miranda and her husband, Morris, lives in Atlanta, Georgia, and are the parents of two adult children, Latrelle and Davin.

CONTACT INFORMATION

For more information or to order books contact:

Miranda Burnette Ministries, Inc.
P. O. Box 314
Clarkdale, GA 30111

E-mail:
miranda@ mirandaburnetteministries.org

Website:
www.mirandaburnetteministries.org

OTHER BOOKS BY MIRANDA BURNETTE

Dare to Dream and Soar Like an Eagle
The Sky is the Limit!

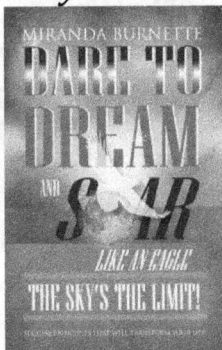

If you are ready to take the challenge to make your dreams a reality, this book is for you. In these pages, Miranda Burnette shares important success principles that will absolutely transform your life. The keys contained in this powerful book will help you soar from level to level in order to fulfill God's purpose for your life.

Dare to Dream and Soar like an Eagle will help you:

- Maximize your potential

- Achieve your goals

- Clarify your vision

- Cultivate inspired ideas

- Release the seeds of greatness that God has placed inside you

- Recognize that God created you for *SUCCESS*

It doesn't matter who you are or what you are experiencing in your life right now, you have residing within you God-given ability to accomplish more than you could ever imagine. So Dare to Dream and Soar Like an Eagle! *The Sky's the Limit!*

Success Starts In Your Mind
A Manual on How to Think Your Way to Success

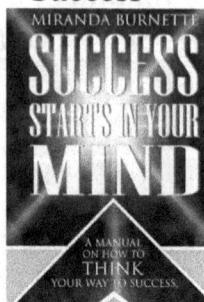

If you could change one thing in your life right now, what would you change? Have you ever considered changing your thoughts? If you are frustrated, discontented, and disappointed with your life, if you want to be successful in different areas of your life, if you want to be freed from the bondage of bad habits, and if you want your life to change, *THIS BOOK IS FOR YOU!* If you want your life to change, you have to change your thinking. Your life won't change unless your thoughts change. You can change your life by changing your thoughts.

Success Starts in Your Mind will help you:

- Understand the power of thoughts
- Develop an understanding of the relationship between success and the mind
- Think positively
- Overcome the fear of success
- Comprehend how what you think about yourself can dramatically affect your level of success
- Realize that *Success Starts In Your Mind*

If you are not successful, or if you are not as successful as you would like to be, it is time for you to start *Thinking Your Way to Success.*

Leader to Leader
Inspiring Words for Women in Leadership

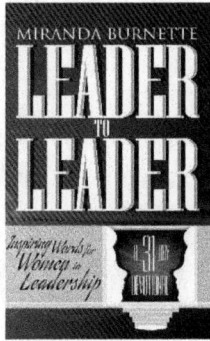

Do you want to be a strong, confident leader?

Do you want to learn leadership principles that will take you and your

organization to the next level?

Do you desire to develop leaders, not just followers?

Do you want to learn how to make good decisions?

THEN THIS BOOK IS FOR YOU!

Leader to Leader will help you to:

Discover how to be an effective leader

Develop principles of leadership that will help you be the leader others

will follow

Learn the qualities of a great leader

Realize that failure is not fatal

Use your past mistakes as a stepping stone to rise to the next level

Lead by example

Develop great leaders

Read, study, and meditate on the leadership principles in this devotional, and become the effective leader you've always wanted to be.

Keys to Living a Fruit-Filled Life
Nine Keys That Will Unlock the Door to Success in Your Life

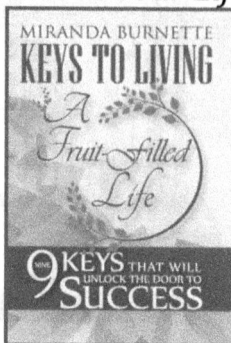

Do you want to have a successful, productive, fulfilling life? Would you like to have a life where you accomplish great things? Have you desired a life where you are constantly growing and over flowing with blessings and prosperity? Do you want a life that is producing good fruit? Would you like to live your life in such a way that you make a great difference in the lives of others? Do you want a life that is full of love, joy, peace, patience, kindness, goodness, humility, faithfulness, and self-control? If you answered yes to all of those questions, *THIS BOOK IS FOR YOU! Keys to Living a Fruit-Filled Life* will teach you:

How to live a happier more peaceful life

How to prepare for great opportunities

Steps to develop the Fruit of the Spirit in your life

How to develop great relationships

Nine keys that will unlock the door to success in your life

How to live the *"Good Life"*

Keys to Living a Fruit-Filled Life will open the door to success in your life and guide you into how to enjoy the abundant life God has for you.

Dare to Dream Again
It's Never too Late For a New Beginning
Book and Study

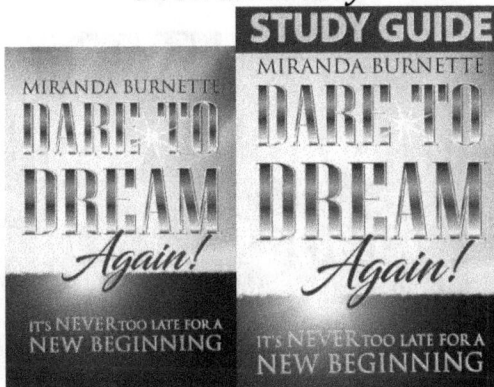

Have you ever dreamed of winning something, being something, or starting something? Maybe you have dreamed of starting your own business, earning a degree, becoming a professional athlete, artist, or musician. We are born dreamers! When you stop dreaming, it seems as if a part of you is missing. Nothing else seems to fulfill you as much as the desire to realize or accomplish your dream.

God has a specific plan designed for each of our lives. Nevertheless, it is our responsibility to stay on the path to our dream. We must hold on to the dream, cooperate with God, and fulfill the plan He has for our lives. If you have lost sight of your dream, and given up on your dream, it is time to dream again! As you read this book, it is my sincere prayer that you will pick up the shattered pieces of your dream and rekindle the passion you once had and *Dare to Dream Again!* Once you start dreaming again, this time, don't let anyone or anything stop you from living your dream! Hold on to your dream and don't let it go!

Winning With the Power of Love
How to Love Your Way to Victory
Book and Study Guide

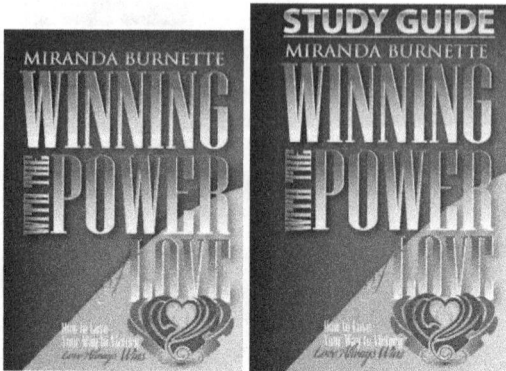

Do you want to be a winner in life? Do you want to reach your goals, be successful, have good relationships, and prosper in every area of your life? Do you want to have joy, peace, and happiness abounding in your life? Do you want to make a difference in the lives of others and help them to succeed and be winners? If your answer to all of these questions is *YES, THIS BOOK IS FOR YOU! Winning With the Power of Love* will help you to be the winner you have always dreamed you could be. This book contains the tools you need to overcome obstacles that have been holding you back and reach your full God-given potential.

Winning With the Power of Love will teach you:

- The true meaning of being a winner
- How the power of love can literally change your life
- How to win with people
- How to win by loving yourself
- Why love is so powerful

- How the force of love will drive fear out of your life forever
- How walking in the power of love can increase your faith
- How many of your problems can be solved by you receiving God's love, loving yourself, loving God and loving others

If you are not loving, you are not winning. You can't lose when you love. Love has never lost a battle and it never will. You can win with the power of love. Start loving and start winning today. Building your life on the solid foundation of love will enable you to accomplish more in life than you could ever imagine.